SWEET WILL

BOOKS BY PHILIP LEVINE

SWEET WILL   1985

SELECTED POEMS   1984

ONE FOR THE ROSE   1981

7 YEARS FROM SOMEWHERE   1979

ASHES: POEMS OLD AND NEW   1979

THE NAMES OF THE LOST   1976

1933   1974

THEY FEED THEY LION   1972

RED DUST   1971

PILI'S WALL   1971

NOT THIS PIG   1968

ON THE EDGE   1963

SWEET WILL

POEMS BY

PHILIP LEVINE

ATHENEUM NEW YORK *1985*

My thanks to the editors of the following magazines in
which these poems first appeared:
COLUMBIA   *(The final section of "Late Light" under the
title "Dutch Light")*
THE IOWA REVIEW   *("Salts and Oils")*
MIDWESTERN POETRY JOURNAL   *("The House")*
THE NEW YORKER   *("An Ordinary Morning" under the
title "One by One," "Last Words," "Late Light,"
the final section of "A Poem with No Ending" under
the title "Shore," "Voyages," "Wisteria," "Those
Were the Days")*
PARIS REVIEW   *("A Poem with No Ending" and "An
Ending")*
PLOUGHSHARES   *("Then")*
POETRY   *("Jewish Graveyards, Italy," "Look," "The
Present," "Sweet Will")*
VANITY FAIR   *("The White Iris")*

Published simultaneously in Canada by McClelland and Stewart Ltd
LCCN *84–45781*
ISBN *0–689–11585–7 (clothbound);* ISBN *0–689–11586–5 (paperback)*
Composed and printed by Heritage Printers, Inc.,
Charlotte, North Carolina
Bound by The Delmar Company, Charlotte, North Carolina
Designed by Harry Ford
First Edition

FOR HARRY FORD

> . . . *silent, bare,*
> *Ships, towers, domes, theatres, and temples lie*
> *Open unto the fields, and to the sky;*
> *All bright and glittering in the smokeless air.*
> *Never did sun more beautifully, steep*
> *In his first splendour, valley, rock, or hill;*
> *Ne'er saw I, never felt, a calm so deep!*
> *The river glideth at his own sweet will . . .*

WORDSWORTH

CONTENTS

I

Voyages	3
Salts and Oils	5
Those Were the Days	7
The White Iris	9
Wisteria	10
Look	11
The Present	13
Sweet Will	17

II

A Poem With No Ending	21

III

An Ending	39
Late Light	41
The House	46
Last Words	47
An Ordinary Morning	50
Then	51
Jewish Graveyards, Italy	53

I

VOYAGES

Pond snipe, bleached pine, rue weed, wart—
I walk by sedge and brown river rot
to where the old lake boats went daily out.
All the ships are gone, the gray wharf fallen
in upon itself. Even the channel's
grown over. Once we set sail here
for Bob-Lo, the Brewery Isles, Cleveland.
We would have gone as far as Niagara
or headed out to open sea if the Captain
said so, but the Captain drank. Blood-eyed
in the morning, coffee shaking in his hand,
he'd plead to be put ashore or drowned,
but no one heard. Enormous in his long coat,
Sinbad would take the helm and shout out
orders swiped from pirate movies. Once
we docked north of Vermillion to meet
a single spur of the old Ohio Western
and sat for days waiting for a train,
waiting for someone to claim the cargo
or give us anything to take back,
like the silver Cadillac roadster
it was rumored we had once freighted
by itself. The others went foraging
and left me with the Captain, locked up
in the head and sober. Two days passed,
I counted eighty tankers pulling
through the flat lake waters on their way,
I counted blackbirds gathering at dusk
in the low trees, clustered like bees.
I counted the hours from noon to noon
and got nowhere. At last the Captain slept.
I banked the fire, raised anchor, cast off,
and jumping ship left her drifting out
on the black bay. I walked seven miles
to the Interstate and caught a meat truck
heading west, and came to over beer,
hashbrowns, and fried eggs in a cafe

northwest of Omaha. I could write
how the radio spoke of war, how
the century was half its age, how
dark clouds gathered in the passes
up ahead, the dispossessed had clogged
the roads, but none the less I alone
made my way to the western waters,
a foreign ship, another life, and disappeared
from all I'd known. In fact I
come home every year, I walk the same streets
where I grew up, but now with my boys.
I settled down, just as you did, took
a degree in library sciences,
and got my present position with
the county. I'm supposed to believe
something ended. I'm supposed to be
dried up. I'm supposed to represent
a yearning, but I like it the way it is.
Not once has the ocean wind changed
and brought the taste of salt
over the coastal hills and through
the orchards to my back yard. Not once
have I wakened cold and scared
out of a dreamless sleep
into a dreamless life and cried
and cried out for what I left behind.

SALTS AND OILS

In Havana in 1948 I ate fried dog
believing it was Peking duck. Later,
in Tampa I bunked with an insane sailor
who kept a .38 Smith and Wesson in his shorts.
In the same room were twins, oilers
from Toledo, who argued for hours
each night whose turn it was
to get breakfast and should he turn
the eggs or not. On the way north
I lived for three days on warm water
in a DC-6 with a burned out radio
on the runway at Athens, Georgia. We sang
a song, "Georgia's Big Behind," and prayed
for WWIII and complete, unconditional surrender.
Napping in an open field near Newport News,
I chewed on grass while the shadows of September
lengthened; in the distance a man hammered
on the roof of a hangar and groaned how he
was out of luck and vittles. Bummed a ride
in from Mitchell Field and had beet borscht
and white bread at 34th and 8th Avenue.
I threw up in the alley behind the YMCA
and slept until they turned me out.
I walked the bridge to Brooklyn
while the East River browned below.
A mile from Ebbetts Field, from all
that history, I found Murray, my papa's
buddy, in his greasy truck shop, polishing
replacement parts. Short, unshaven, puffed,
he strutted the filthy aisles,
a tiny Ghengis Khan. He sent out for soup
and sandwiches. The world turned on barley,
pickled meats, yellow mustard, kasha,
rye breads. It rained in October, rained
so hard I couldn't walk and smoke, so I
chewed pepsin chewing gum. The rain
spoiled Armistice Day in Lancaster, Pa.

The open cars overflowed, girls cried,
the tubas and trombones went dumb,
the floral displays shredded, the gutters
clogged with petals. Afterwards had ham
on buttered whole-wheat bread, ham
and butter for the first time
on the same day in Zanesville with snow
forecast, snow, high winds, closed roads,
solid darkness before 5 p.m. These were not
the labors of Hercules, these were not
of meat or moment to anyone but me
or destined for story or to learn from
or to make me fit to take the hand
of a toad or a toad princess or to stand
in line for food stamps. One quiet morning
at the end of my thirteenth year a little bird
with a dark head and tattered tail feathers
had come to the bedroom window and commanded
me to pass through the winding miles
of narrow dark corridors and passageways
of my growing body the filth and glory
of the palatable world. Since then I've
been going out and coming back
the way a swallow does with unerring grace
and foreknowledge because all of this
was prophesied in the final, unread book
of the Midrash and because I have to
grow up and because it pleases me.

THOSE WERE THE DAYS

The sun came up before breakfast,
perfectly round and yellow, and we
dressed in the soft light and shook out
our long blond curls and waited
for Maid to brush them flat and place
the part just where it belonged.
We came down the carpeted stairs
one step at a time, in single file,
gleaming in our sailor suits, two
four year olds with unscratched knees
and scrubbed teeth. Breakfast came
on silver dishes with silver covers
and was set in table center, and Mother
handed out the portions of eggs
and bacon, toast and juice. We could
hear the ocean, not far off, and boats
firing up their engines, and the shouts
of couples in white on the tennis courts.
I thought, Yes, this is the beginning
of another summer, and it will go on
until the sun tires of us or the moon
rises in its place on a silvered dawn
and no one wakens. My brother flung
his fork on the polished wooden floor
and cried out, "My eggs are cold, cold!"
and turned his plate over. I laughed
out loud, and Mother slapped my face,
and when I cleared my eyes the table
was bare of even a simple white cloth,
and the steaming plates had vanished.
My brother said, "It's time," and we
struggled into our galoshes and snapped
them up, slumped into our pea coats,
one year older now and on our way
to the top through the freezing rains
of the end of November, lunch boxes
under our arms, tight fists pocketed,

out the door and down the front stoop,
heads bent low, tacking into the wind.

THE WHITE IRIS

A single stalk climbed up
to my window to hold out
its long white bud. Late March
under a slow sky, the alder
shudders in the west wind
and stills, even the jays
have quieted.
                Yesterday
just after dawn, I found
my tall son John working
the garden paths. Unable
to sleep he had come home
on foot through the dark town
to take up the shovel
and the hoe.
                 Now the rain
dances on the shed roof, bows
down the wild asparagus,
and blackens the earth. If I
wakened in the stillness
of this afternoon, I'd find
a blue sky and the iris
beaten open into blossom.

WISTERIA

The first purple wisteria
I recall from boyhood hung
on a wire outside the windows
of the breakfast room next door
at the home of Steve Pisaris.
I loved his tall, skinny daughter,
or so I thought, and I would wait
beside the back door, prostrate,
begging to be taken in. Perhaps
it was only the flowers of spring
with their sickening perfumes
that had infected me. When Steve
and Sophie and the three children
packed up and made the move west,
I went on spring after spring,
leaden with desire, half-asleep,
praying to die. Now I know
those prayers were answered.
That boy died, the brick houses
deepened and darkened with rain,
age, use, and finally closed
their eyes and dreamed the sleep
of California. I learned this
only today. Wakened early
in an empty house not lately
battered by storms, I looked
for nothing. On the surface
of the rain barrel, the paled,
shredded blossoms floated.

LOOK

The low-built houses of the poor
were all around him, and it
was dawn now, and he was more
awake than not. So it is
a young man begins his life.
Someone, probably his brother,
has quietly closed the front
door, and he feels a sudden gust
of cold air and opens his eyes.
Through the uncurtained window
the great factory sulks in gray
light, there where his mother
must be finishing the night,
her arms crossed and immersed
in the deep, milky washbasin,
those long and slender arms
that seem to him as hard
and drawn as a man's, and
now she would be smiling
with one eye closed and blurred
by the first cigarette in hours.
He sits up and lights his first
too and draws the smoke in
as deeply as he can and feels
his long nakedness stretched
out before him, filling the bed
now grown too small for him.
They will pass, mother and son,
on the street, and he will hold
her straight, taut body for
a moment and smell the grease
in her hair and touch her lips
with his, and today he will not
wonder why the tears start and
stall in her eyes and in his.
Today for the first time in
his life he will let his hands

stray across her padded back
and shoulders, feeling them
give and then hold, and he will
not say one word, not *mother*
or *Ruth* or *goodbye*. If you
are awake in the poor light
of this November, have a look
down at the street that leads
the way you too will have soon
to take. Do you see them there
stopped in each others' arms,
these two who love each other?
Go ahead and look! You wanted
to live as much as they did,
you asked the day to start,
and the day started, but not
because you asked. Forward
or back, they've got no place
to go. No one's blaming you.

THE PRESENT

The day comes slowly in the railyard
behind the ice factory. It broods on
one cinder after another until each
glows like lead or the eye of a dog
possessed of no inner fire, the brown
and greasy pointer who raises his muzzle
a moment and sighing lets it thud
down on the loading dock. In no time
the day has crossed two sets of tracks,
a semi-trailer with no tractor, and crawled
down three stories of the bottling plant
at the end of the alley. It is now
less than five hours until mid-day
when nothing will be left in doubt,
each scrap of news, each banished carton,
each forgotten letter, its ink bled of lies,
will stare back at the one eye that sees
it all and never blinks. But for now
there is water settling in a clean glass
on the shelf beside the razor, the slap
of bare feet on the floor above. Soon
the scent of rivers borne across roof
after roof by winds without names,
the aroma of opened beds better left
closed, of mouths without teeth, of light
rustling among the mice droppings
at the back of a bin of potatoes.

*

The old man who sleeps among the cases
of empty bottles in a little nest of rags
and newspapers at the back of the plant
is not an old man. He is twenty years
younger than I am now putting this down
in permanent ink on a yellow legal pad
during a crisp morning in October.

When he fell from a high pallet, his sleeve
caught on a nail and spread his arms
like a figure out of myth. His head
tore open on a spear of wood, and he
swore in French. No, he didn't want
a doctor. He wanted toilet paper
and a drink, which were fetched. He used
the tiny bottle of whisky to straighten
out his eyes and the toilet paper to clean
his pants, fouled in the fall, and he did
both with seven teenage boys looking on
in wonder and fear. At last the blood
slowed and caked above his ear, and he
never once touched the wound. Instead,
in a voice no one could hear, he spoke
to himself, probably in French, and smoked
sitting back against a pallet, his legs
thrust out on the damp cement floor.

*

In his white coveralls, crisp and pressed,
Teddy the Polack told us a fat tit
would stop a toothache, two a headache.
He told it to anyone who asked, and grinned—
the small eyes watering at the corners—
as Alcibiades might have grinned
when at last he learned that love leads
even the body beloved to a moment
in the present when desire calms, the skin
glows, the soul takes the light of day,
even a working day in 1944.
For Baharozian at seventeen the present
was a gift. Seeing my ashen face,
the cold sweats starting, he seated me
in a corner of the boxcar and did
both our jobs, stacking the full cases

neatly row upon row and whistling
the songs of Kate Smith. In the bathroom
that night I posed naked before the mirror,
the new cross of hair staining my chest,
plunging to my groin. That was Wednesday,
for every Wednesday ended in darkness.

*

One of those teenage boys was my brother.
That night as we lay in bed, the lights
out, we spoke of Froggy, of how at first
we thought he would die and how little
he seemed to care as the blood rose
to fill and overflow his ear. Slowly
the long day came over us and our breath
quieted and eased at last, and we slept.
When I close my eyes now his bare legs
glow before me again, pure and lovely
in their perfect whiteness, the buttocks
dimpled and firm. I see again the rope
of his sex, unwrinkled, flushed and swaying,
the hard flat belly as he raises his shirt
to clean himself. He gazes at no one
or nothing, but seems instead to look off
into a darkness I hadn't seen, a pool
of shadow that forms before his eyes,
in my memory now as solid as onyx.

*

I began this poem in the present
because nothing is past. The ice factory,
the bottling plant, the cindered yard
all gave way to a low brick building
a block wide and windowless where they
designed gun mounts for personnel carriers

that never made it to Korea. My brother
rises early, and on clear days he walks
to the corner to have toast and coffee.
Seventeen winters have melted into an earth
of stone, bottle caps, and old iron to carry
off the hard remains of Froggy Frenchman
without a blessing or a stone to bear it.
A little spar of him the size of a finger,
pointed and speckled as though blood-flaked,
washed ashore from Lake Erie near Buffalo
before the rest slipped down the falls out
into the St. Lawrence. He could be at sea,
he could be part of an ocean, by now
he could even be home. This morning I
rose later than usual in a great house
full of sunlight, but I believe it came
down step by step on each wet sheet
of wooden siding before it crawled
from the ceiling and touched my pillow
to waken me. When I heave myself
out of this chair with a great groan of age
and stand shakily, the three mice still
in the wall. From across the lots
the wind brings voices I can't make out,
scraps of song or sea sounds, daylight
breaking into dust, the perfume of waiting
rain, of onions and potatoes frying.

SWEET WILL

The man who stood beside me
34 years ago this night fell
on to the concrete, oily floor
of Detroit Transmission, and we
stepped carefully over him until
he wakened and went back to his press.

It was Friday night, and the others
told me that every Friday he drank
more than he could hold and fell
and he wasn't any dumber for it
so just let him get up at his
own sweet will or he'll hit you.

"At his own sweet will," was just
what the old black man said to me,
and he smiled the smile of one
who is still surprised that dawn
graying the cracked and broken windows
could start us all to singing in the cold.

Stash rose and wiped the back of his head
with a crumpled handkerchief and looked
at his own blood as though it were
dirt and puzzled as to how
it got there and then wiped the ends
of his fingers carefully one at a time

the way the mother wipes the fingers
of a sleeping child, and climbed back
on his wooden soda-pop case to
his punch press and hollered at all
of us over the oceanic roar of work,
addressing us by our names and nations—

"Nigger, Kike, Hunky, River Rat,"
but he gave it a tune, an old tune,
like "America the Beautiful." And he danced
a little two-step and smiled showing
the four stained teeth left in the front
and took another suck of cherry brandy.

In truth it was no longer Friday,
for night had turned to day as it
often does for those who are patient,
so it was Saturday in the year of '48
in the very heart of the city of man
where your Cadillac cars get manufactured.

In truth all those people are dead,
they have gone up to heaven singing
"Time on My Hands" or "Begin the Beguine,"
and the Cadillacs have all gone back
to earth, and nothing that we made
that night is worth more than me.

And in truth I'm not worth a thing
what with my feet and my two bad eyes
and my one long nose and my breath
of old lies and my sad tales of men
who let the earth break them back,
each one, to dirty blood or bloody dirt.

Not worth a thing! Just like it was said
at my magic birth when the stars
collided and fire fell from great space
into great space, and people rose one
by one from cold beds to tend a world
that runs on and on at its own sweet will.

II

A POEM WITH NO ENDING

So many poems begin where they
should end, and never end.
Mine never end, they run on
book after book, complaining
to the moon that heaven is wrong
or dull, no place at all to be.
I believe all this. I believe
that ducks take wing only
in stories and then to return
the gift of flight to the winds.
If you knew how I came to be
seven years old and how thick
and blond my hair was, falling
about my shoulders like the leaves
of the slender eucalyptus
that now blesses my driveway
and shades my pale blue Falcon,
if you could see me pulling
wagon loads of stones across
the tufted fields and placing
them to build myself and my brother
a humped mound of earth where
flowers might rise as from a grave,
you might understand the last spring
before war turned toward our house
and entered before dawn, a pale
stranger that hovered over each bed
and touched the soft, unguarded faces
leaving bruises so faint
years would pass before they darkened
and finally burned. Now I can sit
calmly over coffee and recover
each season, how the rains swelled
the streets, how at night I mumbled
a prayer because the weight
of snow was too great to bear
as I heard it softly packing

down the roof, how I waited
for hours for some small breeze
to rise from the river dreaming
beside me, and none came, and morning
was so much mist rising
and the long moaning of the ore boats
returning the way they'd come,
only now freighted with the earth
someone would carve and cook.
That is the poem I called "Boyhood"
and placed between the smeared pages
of your morning paper. White itself,
it fell on the white tablecloth
and meant so little you turned
it over and wrote a column
of figures you never added up.
You capped your gold fountain pen
and snapped your fingers to remind
yourself of some small, lost event.
My poem remained long after you'd
gone, face down, unread, not even
misunderstood, until it passed,
like its subject, into the literatures
of silence, though hardly first
among them, for there have always
been the tales the water told
the cup and the words the wind
sang to the windows in those houses
we abandoned after the roads
whispered all night in our ears.

*

I passed the old house and saw
even from the front that four trees
were gone, and beside the drive
a wire cage held nothing. Once

I stopped and rang the bell.
A woman said, No! before I asked,
and I heard a child say, Who
is he? and I turned away
from so many years and drove off.
Tomorrow my train will leave
the tunnel and rise above this town
and slowly clatter beside block
after block of buildings that fall
open like so many stunned faces
with nothing to hide. The cold odor
of smoke rises and the steeped smell
of wood that will not hold our words.
Once I saw the back of a closet
that burst into sky, and I imagined
opening a familiar door and stepping
into a little room without limits.
I rose into a blue sky as undefined
as winter and as cold. I said, Oh my!
and held myself together with a wish.
No, that wasn't childhood, that
was something else, something
that ended in a single day and left
no residue of happiness I could
reach again if I took the first turn
to the left and eyes closed walked
a hundred and one steps and spoke
the right words.

*

I sit for days
staring at the dusty window
and no word comes to tell me what I
left behind. Still, I regret nothing,
not the little speeches I wrote
to the moon on the warm spring nights

I searched for someone other
than myself and came home empty
at sunup among bird calls
and the faint prattle of rain.
I do not regret my hands
changing before me, mottling
like the first eggs I found
in the fields of junked cars,
nor my breath that still comes
and comes no matter what I command
and the words that go out
and fall short. I can hear
my heart beating, slowly,
I can feel the blood sliding
behind my eyes, so I close them
first on a known darkness and then
on a red crown forming as from
a dark sea, and I am beginning
once more to rise into the shape
of someone I can be, a man
no different from my father
but slower and wiser. What could be
better than to waken as a man?

*

I began as you did, smaller
than the wren who circled three times
and flew back into the darkness
before sleep. I was born
of the promise that each night
made and each day broke, out
of the cat's sullen wish to remain
useless and proud and the sunlight's
to find a closed face to waken.
Out of just that and no more.
The tiny stories my grandpa

told in which dogs walked upright
and the dead laughed. I was born
of these and his pocket of keys,
his dresser drawers of black socks
and white shirts, his homilies
of blood and water, all he never
gave me and all he did. Small
and dying he opened his eyes
to a certain day, to
stale water and old shoes,
and he never prayed. I could say
that was the finished poem and gather
my few things into a dark suitcase
and go quietly into the streets and wait.
It will be Sunday, and no one will pass.
In the long shadows of the warehouses
it's cool and pleasant. A piece of paper
skips by, but I don't bend to it
or tip my hat.

*

           I hear the shouts
of children at play. Sunday afternoon
in August of '36, and the darkness
falls between us on the little island
where we came year after year
to celebrate the week. First I can't
see you, my brother, but I can hear
your labored breathing beside me,
and then my legs vanish, and then
my hands, and I am only a presence
in long grass. Then I am grass
blowing in a field all night, giving
and taking so many green gifts
of the earth and touching everything.
The island still rides the river

between two countries. The playground
—yellowed and shrunken—, the rotunda
falling in upon itself, the old
huddled at separate tables and staring
off into the life they've come to.
In this place and at this time,
which is not time, I could take
the long road back and find it all.
I could even find myself. (Writing
this, I know it's not true.)

*

On Monday morning across the way
the trucks load up with parcels
of everything. This is New York City
in mid-May of 1981, and I am too old
to live that life again, packing
the van with frozen fish, household
goods, oriental vegetables, wristwatches,
weightless cartons of radium. That was
thirty years ago in another town,
and I still recall the mixture
of weariness and excitement as I beheld
the little mound of what was mine
to take into the world. (They had given
me a cap with a shining badge
and a huge revolver to guard
"the valuables." I hid them both
under the seat.) On the near West Side
in a two-room walk-up apartment
a dazed couple sat waiting for weeks
for a foot locker full of clothes
and kitchen utensils. They stood back
when I entered, pretending to be busy,
and they tried to keep me there,
but they had nothing to say. They were

neither young nor old, and I couldn't
then imagine their days in which little
or nothing was done, days on which it
seemed important to smoke before
dressing and not to go out until
late afternoon. I couldn't imagine
who they were and why they'd come
from all the small far-off places
to be homeless where I was homeless.
In another house an old man summoned
me to a high room. There before us
was a massive steamer trunk full
of books he could take back home
to Germany now he could return.
Tolstoi, Balzac, Goethe, all
in the original. Oh yes, I knew
the names, and he called down
to his wife, how wonderful!
This boy knows the names. He brought
the top down carefully, turned the key,
and stepped back, waiting for me
to carry it down three flights
by myself and offered me money
when I couldn't budge it, as though
I'd been pretending. This boy,
this American, in his pressed
work clothes, surely he could do it,
surely there was a way, if only
I would try. I left him shaking
his great head and passed his wife
on the stairs, a little brown mouse
of a woman laughing at such folly.

*

The memory of rain falling slowly
into the dark streets and the smell

of a new season rising above
the trucks parked in silent rows.
Even without earth or snow melting
or new grass rising into moonlight,
the year is turning, and the streets
can feel it. I dreamed this,
or I lived it for a moment, waking
in the night to no bird song
or wind pull, waking to no one
beside me asking for water
or a child calling from another room.
Awake now for a second or a lifetime,
I'm once again stepping out onto
the tiny veranda above the railyards
of Sevilla. In the room next door
a soldier has dressed a chair
with his uniform and leaned his rifle
against the glass door. A woman's clothes
are scattered on the floor. I look away.
Christmas, 1965. The halls of this hotel
are filled with sleeping peasants.
Each of my three sons is alone
in a narrow room with no windows,
asleep in a darkness beyond darkness,
and I feel their loneliness and fear.
Below the window, the lights
of the railyard flash this way
and that, and an old engine is firing up.
Distant voices speak out, but I can't
understand their words. I am falling
toward sleep again. For a moment
I feel my arms spread wide to enclose
everyone within these walls whitewashed
over and over, my own sons, my woman,
and all the other sons and daughters
stretched out or curled up in bad beds
or on bare floors, their heads

pillowed on their own hard arms,
their cheeks darkened by cheap newsprint.
There is a song, bird song or wind song,
or the song old rooms sing when no one
is awake to hear. For a moment I
almost catch the melody we make
with bare walls, old iron sagging beds,
and scarred floors. There is one
deep full note for each of us.
This is the first night of my life
I know we are music.

      *

                          Across the world
in the high mountains of the West,
I had gone one Sunday
with my youngest son, Teddy.
We parked the car and climbed
from the road's end over a rise
of young pines and then descended
slowly for a mile or more
through a meadow of wildflowers
still blooming in July. The yellow
ones that reached to his shoulders
stained my legs with pollen.
As we walked he spoke of animals
with the gift of speech. Bears,
he told me, were especially fond
of young people, and the mother bears
were known for coming into towns
like ours to steal boys and girls
and bring them back up here and teach
them hunting, and the children
grew into animals and forgot
their homes and their brothers.
A slight rise, and we entered

a thick forest. The air was still
and damp, and there was no longer
any trail. Soon I lost my way.
In a small clearing we stopped
to have our sandwiches, and I cooled
the soda pop in a stream whose rushing
we'd heard from far off. His head
pillowed on his jacket, he lay out,
eyes closed, the long dark lashes
quivering in sunlight, the cheeks
brown and smooth. When I awoke
he was throwing rocks as large
as he could manage into the stream
where they banged down a stairway
of stone and came to rest. The sun
had shifted, the shadows fell
across our faces, and it was cooler.
He was building a house, he said,
below the water, dark now, and boiling.
I bet him he couldn't lead us back
the way we'd come through the dark
bear woods and across the great plain
and up and down these hills.
A dollar? he said. Yes. And talking
all the way, he took the lead,
switching a fallen branch before him
to dub this little tree as friend
or a tall weed as enemy, stopping once
to uproot a purple wildflower for me.

*

I reenter a day in a late summer,
the heat going from the streets
and the cramped downriver flats, a day
of departures and farewells, for I
too am going, packing my box

of books and my typewriter and heading
West this time. So it seems
that all of us are on the move,
giving up these jobs that gave us
just enough and took all we had.
Going back to the little hollows
we'd come away from when the land
gave out or going back
to the survivors left in Alabama
or farther back to the villages
of Greece and Italy. From all
of these people I take a drink,
a pastry, and a coin to insure
a safe voyage, and we shake hands
around the battered kitchen tables.
Sometimes the old ones turn away
before I leave and cry without sound
or sometimes a man touches
his wife, but more often each stands
alone and silent in the old pain.

*

How many lives were torn apart
in those years? How many young men
went off as ours did but never
came back? It was still dark when we
drove into the great harbor and found
the ship to Sweden and said goodbye
not knowing what it was we said.
We saw him climb the gangplank
loaded down with duffle bags
and a guitar he scarcely played.
We turned back to the city
unable to face each other,
unable to face the coming day.
The sun shone on trams and markets,

and until late afternoon I tramped
the streets no longer looking for
the face I sought in childhood,
for now that face was mine, and I
was old enough to know
that my son would not suddenly
turn a corner and be mine
as I was my father's son.
A woman came out of a bar
screaming at her man, and he
hurried silently beside me
and darted quickly down an alley.
When I turned the woman's face
was smeared with tears. She shook
a finger at me and damned me
in her tongue. That night I
slept alone and dreamed of finding
my way back to the house where I
was born. It was quiet when I
entered, for no one had risen yet,
and I climbed the steps to my room
where nothing stirred in all
the rooms beneath me. I slept
fully dressed, stretched out
on a tiny bed, a boy's bed,
and in that dream more vivid
than the waking from it, the rooms
were one and I was home at last.

*

To get west you go east.
You leave in the dark
by car and drive until you
can't and sleep by the road
for an hour or a moment.
If the windshield is crystalled

when you waken you know
the days will be getting
colder and shorter. If you
wake soaked with sweat
then the year is turning
toward summer. None of
it matters at all, the towns
you travel through, plunging
down hills and over the cobbles
and the twisting tight passageways
and breaking for the open fields,
the apple orchards and the barns
rotting and fallen, none of it
matters to you. No one
you know dreams these houses
or hides here from the rain.
When the long day turns
to dark and you're nowhere
you've ever been before, you
keep going, and the magic eyes
that gleam by the roadside
are those of animals come
down from the invisible hills.
Yes, they have something to tell
or something to give you
from a world you've lost.
If you stopped the car and let
the engine idle and walked
slowly toward them, one hand
held out in greeting, you
would find only a fence post
bullet-scarred and deckled with
red-eyed reflectors. None
of it matters, so just keep going,
forward or back, until you've
found the place or the place
doesn't matter. They were only

animals come down to stand
in silent formation by a road
you traveled.

*

We sat by the shore
together as the sea rose in sharp
waves and turned a darker blue.
The families around us shook out
their blankets and gathered up
what remained of their meals
under the sun. A sea wind blew
in and tore their words away and set
the sand to twisting about us.
When my eyes stopped watering
sky and sea were one black cloth
broken by no light, and we walked
back to the little unlighted station
where the dark-eyed children dozed
on benches beside their mothers.
The cars were crowded. The train
stopped at each sea town to pick up
the last stragglers, and we stood
pressed together, groaning, as we
jarred and jolted over the old track
and finally entered the black tunnel
that led to the center of the city.
In the plaza young couples whispered
together and soldiers passed in pairs,
armed and silent, their faces
glistening between the heavy wool
of cap and tunic. We walked the long
avenue back to our room, back to
the empty crippled bed that held
a place for us. Now this is home,
I thought, now I live nowhere

and have made friends with the seas
that work even while I sleep. I
see in the ocean of my memory
the shore birds going out and nothing
coming back. No light enters
the little room, but I can hear
the unsteady tapping of an old man
going home and the young starting
out for work. It's Monday morning
now, and their harsh voices rise
calling out to each other or
to no one in cries or in songs
that fill my sleep. I see beyond
the dark the distant sky breaking
into color and each wave taking
shape and rising landward.

III

AN ENDING

Early March.
The cold beach deserted. My kids
home in a bare house, bundled up
and listening to rock music
pirated from England. My wife
waiting for me in a bar, alone
for an hour over her sherry, and none
of us knows why I have to pace
back and forth on this flat
and birdless stretch of gleaming sand
while the violent air shouts
out its rags of speech. I recall
the calm warm sea of Florida
30 years ago, and my brother
and I staring out in the hope
that someone known and loved
would return out of air and water
and no more, a miracle a kid
could half-believe, could see
as something everyday and possible.
Later I slept alone and dreamed
of the home I never had and wakened
in the dark. A silver light sprayed
across the bed, and the little
rented room ticked toward dawn.
I did not rise. I did not go
to the window and address
the moon. I did not cry
or cry out against the hour
or the loneliness that still
was mine, for I had grown
into the man I am, and I
knew better. A sudden voice
calls out my name or a name
I think is mine. I turn.
The waves have darkened; the sky's
descending all around me. I read

once that the sea would come
to be the color of heaven.
They would be two seas tied
together, and between the two
a third, the sea of my own heart.
I read and believed nothing.
This little beach at the end
of the world is anywhere, and I
stand in a stillness that will last
forever or until the first light
breaks beyond these waters. Don't
be scared, the book said, don't flee
as wave after wave the breakers rise
in darkness toward their ghostly crests,
for he has set a limit to the sea
and he is at your side. The sea
and I breathe in and out as one.
Maybe this is done at last
or for now, this search for what
is never here. Maybe all that
ancient namesake sang is true.
The voice I hear now is
my own night voice, going out
and coming back in an old chant
that calms me, that calms
—for all I know—the waves
still lost out there.

LATE LIGHT

Rain filled the streets
once a year, rising almost
to door and window sills,
battering walls and roofs
until it cleaned away the mess
we'd made. My father told
me this, he told me it ran
downtown and spilled into
the river, which in turn
emptied finally into the sea.
He said this only once
while I sat on the arm
of his chair and stared out
at the banks of gray snow
melting as the March rain
streaked past. All the rest
of that day passed on
into childhood, into nothing,
or perhaps some portion hung
on in a tiny corner of thought.
Perhaps a clot of cinders
that peppered the front yard
clung to a spar of old weed
or the concrete lip of the curb
and worked its way back under
the new growth spring brought
and is a part of that yard
still. Perhaps light falling
on distant houses becomes
those houses, hunching them
down at dusk like sheep
browsing on a far hillside,
or at daybreak gilds
the roofs until they groan
under the new weight, or
after rain lifts haloes
of steam from the rinsed,

white aluminum siding,
and those houses and all
they contain live that day
in the sight of heaven.

II

In the blue, winking light
of the International Institute
of Social Revolution
I fell asleep one afternoon
over a book of memoirs
of a Spanish priest who'd
served his own private faith
in a long forgotten war.
An Anarchist and a Catholic,
his remembrances moved
inexplicably from Castilian
to Catalan, a language I
couldn't follow. That dust,
fine and gray, peculiar
to libraries, slipped
between the glossy pages
and my sight, a slow darkness
calmed me, and I forgot
the agony of those men
I'd come to love, forgot
the battles lost and won,
forgot the final trek
over hopeless mountain roads,
defeat, surrender, the vows
to live on. I slept until
the lights came on and off.
A girl was prodding my arm,
for the place was closing.
A slender Indonesian girl

in sweater and American jeans,
her black hair falling
almost to my eyes, she told
me in perfect English
that I could come back,
and she swept up into a folder
the yellowing newspaper stories
and photos spilled out before
me on the desk, the little
chronicles of death themselves
curling and blurring
into death, and took away
the book still unfinished
of a man more confused
even than I, and switched off
the light, and left me alone.

I I I

In June of 1975 I wakened
one late afternoon in Amsterdam
in a dim corner of a library.
I had fallen asleep over a book
and was roused by a young girl
whose hand lay on my hand.
I turned my head up and stared
into her brown eyes, deep
and gleaming. She was crying.
For a second I was confused
and started to speak, to offer
some comfort or aid, but I
kept still, for she was crying
for me, for the knowledge
that I had wakened to a life
in which loss was final.
I closed my eyes a moment.

When I opened them she'd gone,
the place was dark. I went
out into the golden sunlight;
the cobbled streets gleamed
as after rain, the street cafes
crowded and alive. Not
far off the great bell
of the Westerkirk tolled
in the early evening. I thought
of my oldest son, who years
before had sailed from here
into an unknown life in Sweden,
a life which failed, of how
he'd gone alone to Copenhagen,
Bremen, where he'd loaded trains,
Hamburg, Munich, and finally
—sick and weary—he'd returned
to us. He slept in a corner
of the living room for days,
and woke gaunt and quiet,
still only seventeen, his face
in its own shadows. I thought
of my father on the run
from an older war, and wondered
had he passed through Amsterdam,
had he stood, as I did now,
gazing up at the pale sky,
distant and opaque, for the sign
that never comes. Had he drifted
in the same winds of doubt
and change to another continent,
another life, a family, some
years of peace, an early death.
I walked on by myself for miles
and still the light hung on
as though the day would
never end. The gray canals

darkened slowly, the sky
above the high, narrow houses
deepened into blue, and one
by one the stars began
their singular voyages.

THE HOUSE

This poem has a door, a locked door,
and curtains drawn against the day,
but at night the lights come on, one
in each room, and the neighbors swear
they hear music and the sound of dancing.
These days the neighbors will swear
to anything, but that is not why
the house is locked up and no one goes
in or out all day long; that is because
this is a poem first and a house only
at night when everyone should be asleep.
The milkman tries to stop at dawn,
for he has three frosty white bottles
to place by the back door, but his horse
shakes his head back and forth, and so
he passes on his way. The papers pile
up on the front porch until the rain
turns them into gray earth, and they run
down the stairs and say nothing
to anyone. Whoever made this house
had no idea of beauty—it's all gray—
and no idea of what a happy family
needs on a day in spring when tulips
shout from their brown beds in the yard.
Back there the rows are thick with weeds,
stickers, choke grass, the place has gone
to soggy mulch, and the tools are hanging
unused from their hooks in the tool room.
Think of a marriage taking place at one
in the afternoon on a Sunday in June
in the stuffy front room. The dining table
is set for twenty, and the tall glasses
filled with red wine, the silver sparkling.
But no one is going in or out, not even
a priest in his long white skirt, or a boy
in pressed shorts, or a plumber with a fat bag.

LAST WORDS

If the shoe fell from the other foot
who would hear? If the door
opened onto a pure darkness
and it was no dream? If your life
ended the way a book ends
with half a blank page and the survivors
gone off to Africa or madness?
If my life ended in late spring
of 1964 while I walked alone
back down the mountain road?
I sing an old song to myself. I study
the way the snow remains, gray
and damp, in the deep shadows of the firs.
I wonder if the bike is safe hidden
just off the highway. Up ahead
the road, black and winding, falls
away, and there is the valley where
I lived half of my life, spectral
and calm. I sigh with gratitude,
and then I feel an odd pain rising
through the back of my head,
and my eyes go dark. I bend forward
and place my palms on something rough,
the black asphalt or a field of stubble,
and the movement is that of the penitent
just before he stands to his full height
with the knowledge of his enormity.
For that moment which will survive
the burning of all the small pockets
of fat and oil that are the soul,
I am the soul stretching into
the furthest reaches of my fingers
and beyond, glowing like ten candles
in the vault of night for anyone
who could see, even though it is
12:40 in the afternoon and I
have passed from darkness into sunlight

so fierce the sweat streams down
into my eyes. I did not rise.
A wind or a stray animal or a group
of kids dragged me to the side
of the road and turned me over
so that my open eyes could flood heaven.
My clothes went skittering down
the road without me, ballooning
out into any shape, giddy
with release. My coins, my rings,
the keys to my house shattered
like ice and fell into the mountain
thorns and grasses, little bright points
that make you think there is magic
in everything you see. No, it can't
be, you say, for someone is speaking
calmly to you in a voice you know.
Someone alive and confident has put
each of these words down exactly
as he wants them on the page.
You have lived through years
of denial, of public lies, of death
falling like snow on any head
it chooses. You're not a child.
You know the real thing. I am
here, as I always was, faithful
to a need to speak even when all
you hear is a light current of air
tickling your ear. Perhaps.
But what if that dried bundle
of leaves and dirt were not dirt
and leaves but the spent wafer
of a desire to be human? Stop the car,
turn off the engine, and stand
in the silence above your life. See
how the grass mirrors fire, how
a wind rides up the hillside

steadily toward you until it surges
into your ears like breath coming
and going, released from its bondage
to blood or speech and denying nothing.

AN ORDINARY MORNING

A man is singing on the bus
coming in from Toledo.
His voice floats over the heads
that bow and sway with each
turn, jolt, and sudden slowing.
A hoarse, quiet voice, it tells
of love that is true, of love
that endures a whole weekend.
The driver answers in a tenor
frayed from cigarettes, coffee,
and original curses thrown
down from his seat of command.
He answers that he has time
on his hands and it's heavy.
O heavy hangs the head, he
improvises, and the man
back in the very last row,
bouncing now on the cobbles
as we bump down the boulevard,
affirms that it is hanging,
yes, and that it is heavy.
This is what I waken to.
One by one my near neighbors
open their watering eyes
and close their mouths to accept
this bright, sung conversation
on the theme of their morning.
The sun enters from a cloud
and shatters the wide windshield
into seventeen distinct shades
of yellow and fire, the brakes
gasp and take hold, and we are
the living, newly arrived
in Detroit, city of dreams,
each on his own black throne.

THEN

A solitary apartment house, the last one
before the boulevard ends and a dusty road
winds its slow way out of town. On the third floor
through the dusty windows Karen beholds
the elegant couples walking arm in arm
in the public park. It is Saturday afternoon,
and she is waiting for a particular young man
whose name I cannot now recall, if name
he ever had. She runs the thumb of her left hand
across her finger tips and feels the little tags
of flesh the needle made that morning at work
and wonders if he will feel them. She loves her work,
the unspooling of the wide burgundy ribbons
that tumble across her lap, the delicate laces,
the heavy felts for winter, buried now that spring
is rising in the trees. She recalls a black hat
hidden in a deep drawer in the back of the shop.
She made it in February when the snows piled
as high as her waist, and the river stopped at noon,
and she thought she would die. She had tried it on,
a small, close-fitting cap, almost nothing,
pinned down at front and back. Her hair tumbled
out at the sides in dark rags. When she turned
it around, the black felt cupped her forehead
perfectly, the teal feathers trailing out behind,
twin cool jets of flame. Suddenly he is here.
As she goes to the door, the dark hat falls back
into the closed drawer of memory to wait
until the trees are bare and the days shut down
abruptly at five. They touch, cheek to cheek,
and only there, both bodies stiffly arched apart.
As she draws her white gloves on, she can smell
the heat rising from his heavy laundered shirt,
she can almost feel the weight of the iron
hissing across the collar. It's cool out, he says,
cooler than she thinks. There are tiny dots
of perspiration below his hairline. What a day

for strolling in the park! Refusing the chair
by the window, he seems to have no time,
as though this day were passing forever,
although it is barely after two of a late May
afternoon a whole year before the modern era.
Of course she'll take a jacket, she tells him,
of course she was planning to, and she opens her hands,
the fingers spread wide to indicate the enormity
of his folly, for she has on only a blouse,
protection against nothing. In the bedroom
she considers a hat, something dull and proper
as a rebuke, but shaking out her glowing hair
she decides against it. The jacket is there,
the arms spread out on the bed, the arms
of a dressed doll or a soldier at attention
or a boy modelling his first suit, my own arms
when at six I stood beside my sister waiting
to be photographed. She removes her gloves
to feel her balled left hand pass through the silk
of the lining, and then her right, fingers open.
As she buttons herself in, she watches
a slow wind moving through the planted fields
behind the building. She stops and stares.
What was that dark shape she saw a moment
trembling between the sheaves? The sky lowers,
the small fat cypresses by the fields' edge
part, and something is going. Is that the way
she too must take? The world blurs before her eyes
or her sight is failing. I cannot take her hand,
then or now, and lead her to a resting place
where our love matters. She stands frozen
before the twenty-third summer of her life,
someone I know, someone I will always know.

JEWISH GRAVEYARDS, ITALY

dust

Within a low wall falling away
into dust, a few acres of stones,
wildflowers, tall grasses, weeds.
By the house, firewood stacked
neatly for the winter ahead. Now
it is summer, and even before noon
the heat is rising to stun us all,
the crickets, salamanders, ants.
The large, swart flies circle slowly
in air around something I can't see
and won't be waved away. The old man
who answered the bell and let me in
has gone back to his rocking chair
and sits bareheaded softly whistling
a song I've forgotten. Dove moans,
or something like them, from under
the low, scorched pines, and farther
off the laughter of other birds,
and beyond the birds, the hum
of a distant world still there.
A truck gearing down to enter town,
an auto horn, perhaps the voices
of children leaving school, for it's
almost that time. A low wind
raises the hankie I've knotted
at the corners, and with one hand
I hold it and bend to the names
and say them as slowly as I can.
Full, majestic, vanished names
that fill my mouth and go out
into the densely yellowed air
of this great valley and dissolve
as even the sea dissolves beating
on a stone shore or as love does
when the beloved turns to stone

or dust or water. The old man
rocks and whistles by turns
into the long afternoon, and I
bow again to what I don't know.

shade

Wild roses bursting
in the branches of low hemlocks, thistles
to which the bees swarm.
I've come out of the heat of the city to rest
in the shade of death,
but at noon there's no more shade in this place
than on the streets.
As for death, I saw only a huge symbolic spider
that refused to scuttle
into a bin of firewood when I snapped my hankie.
The wood was green olive,
the twisting branches stacked in two-foot lengths.
Once upon a time
when even the weather proved too much, I would
close my eyes and find
another weather. The raw azures and corals
of the soul raged across
the great, black pastures of my childhood
at their pleasure.
That was prayer. But now when I open them
I don't find the grave
of the unknown English poet the world scorned
or his friend who lived,
I don't hear the music of a farther life beyond
this life. I hear traffic
not far off. I see small wild daisies climbing
the weeds that sprout
from the grave of Sofia Finzi Hersch, who died
in New Jersey and rests

among her Italian relatives. I feel my legs
cramp in this odd posture,
for I'm kneeling. I feel the cold damp of soil
given back to the earth
before the earth could take it back, and the heat
familiar on my back
bowed in the poor shade of a rusting alder.

rain

At the end of a street of rain
there's always a place to find,
a gray rope to pull, a dull ringing
from within, an old frowning woman
shuffling in felt house slippers
to unlock the gate and say nothing.
A rusted barrow in an alcove,
shovels crossed on mounded dirt,
then the sad acres of polished stones
fallen this way and that. I can
stand under an umbrella, a man
in a romance I never finished
come to tell the rain a secret
the living don't want and the dead know:
how life goes on, how seasons pass,
the children grow, and the earth gives
back what it took. My shoes darken.
I move from one cluster of stones
to another studying the names
and dates that tell me nothing I
hadn't guessed. In sunlight, in moonlight,
or in rain, it's always the same,
whatever truth falls from the sky
as slowly as dust settling in
morning light or cold mist rising
from a river, takes the shape

I give it, and I can't give it any.
A wind will come up if I stand
here long enough and blow the clouds
into smoking shapes of water
and earth. Before the last darkness
rises from the wet wild grasses,
new soft rays of late sunlight
will fall through, promising nothing.
They overflow the luminous thorns
of the roses, they catch fire
for a moment on the young leaves.